In the Spirit of the Buddha

Other titles by Paul R. Fleischman

Books, eBooks, and Audiobooks

Vipassana Meditation and the Scientific Worldview - 2nd Edition (2020)
Our Best and Most Lasting Gift (2016)
A Practical and Spiritual Path (2015)
Wonder: When and Why the World Appears Radiant (2013)
An Ancient Path (2009)
Masala Mala (2007)
Cultivating Inner Peace (2004)
You Can Never Speak Up Too Often for the Love of All Things (2004)
The Buddha Taught Nonviolence, Not Pacifism (2002)
Karma & Chaos (1999)
The Healing Spirit: Explorations in Religion and Psychotherapy (1994)
Spiritual Aspects of Psychiatric Practice (1993)

Audio and Video Presentations

A Conversation with Paul R. Fleischman about Vipassana Meditation
and the Scientific Worldview - 2nd Edition (2021)
The Power of Small Changes: Establishing a Daily Vipassana Practice (2021)
Meditating in Troubled Times (2020)
An Introduction to Vipassana Meditation (2020)
Meditation for Adaptive Resilience (2019)
Who We Are and Why We Are the Way We Are (2019)
Meditation for Health Care Professionals (2016)
Don't Use Your Meditation Practice to Harm Yourself (2015)
Spiritual Emotions (2000)
Timeless Mountains, Ceaseless Change (1998)

For many of these titles, visit Pariyatti.
https://store.pariyatti.org/paul_fleischman

In the Spirit of the Buddha

Paul R. and Susan K. Fleischman

Pariyatti Press

Pariyatti Press
An imprint of
Pariyatti Publishing
www.pariyatti.org

First Edition, 2021
ISBN: 978-1-68172-281-8 (Print)
ISBN: 978-1-68172-380-8 (PDF)
ISBN: 978-1-68172-282-5 (ePub)
ISBN: 978-1-68172-353-2 (Mobi)
LCCN: 2021933607

Front and back cover photography by Jeannine Henebry
www.jeanninehenebry.com

Special thanks to Nalin Ariyarathne, Kevin Nash,
Brihas Sarathy, and Steve Hanlon.

Introduction

This collection of prose poems is based upon the teaching of the Buddha. The selections have been chosen for inspiration, rather than representing the full span of the teaching. We have previously presented them as slides, or read them aloud to friends, on various occasions, such as after workshops, following assistant teacher meetings, around fireplaces in national parks, or after evening metta. They have consistently been received with appreciation, and have evoked multiple requests for their publication.

All of these compositions combine the Buddha's thoughts with contemporary phrasing. They cannot be considered direct quotes from the Pali Canon, because we have worked only with English language translations, and because we have combined similar passages, or modified the language for readability. But at the same time, we can't claim that these words are original to us, because they are in the spirit of the Buddha. They are brief, poetic, re-speaking of some of the Buddha's most important ideas. They are sparks from the campfire that continue to glow in the dark.

Our intention is that these slides, or pages, will inspire meditators and non-meditators alike. They are written from the authentic experience of the troubling human condition, and they speak from the standpoint of suffering and the Path out of suffering. They are insights that have crossed the bridge of time from ancient India to today.

We hope you will find wisdom flowing through time on the river of words that originates in the ancient spring of the Pali Canon.

—Paul R. and Susan K. Fleischman

Pebbles thrown by the Buddha thousands of years ago
are now landing in the pools of our minds.

Within our own body we can locate all the laws of nature,
the origin of the world,
the end of the world, and the Path itself.

The feeling of grief follows us around like a starving village dog.
Every person or situation that we love changes and disappears.
This is the origin of "dukkha,"
our dissatisfaction with the world.

Don't cling to anything.
When you understand that, you understand everything.

We find happiness when we discard the belief
that we own ourselves and are in charge of the world.
We can make choices,
but we cannot hold onto everything.
In any moment that we slip free from
grasping
we become unburdened.

The Buddha called freedom from grasping,
"Unshakeable Deliverance."

Wise people speak in a manner that is
clear, personal, profound,
and in a calming and soothing voice.
Their sublime words seem to descend from above,
or to rise up from deep truths
that will be intelligible to other good hearted people.
Wise people can explain Dhamma either briefly or in detail,
revealing their wisdom in speech
that is appealing and helpful.

When you meditate,
effort, concentration, or equanimity
have to be stressed differently from moment to moment.
Strident effort can become wearying.
Concentration emerges in its own time.
Trying to squeeze yourself into equanimity
will only frustrate you.
Meditating in this way is like a goldsmith
who must watch, heat, or cool the gold he is purifying,
so that it emerges pliant and bright,
ready to make any ornament he wants.
He neither overheats it, nor lets it become tepid.

The strings of a guitar play well
only after they have been adjusted to be
neither too loose nor too tight.
Balance your efforts in life and in meditation,
neither forcing them nor letting them sag.
Keep concentration and equanimity in relaxed tension,
like the tuned string.

As a spring-fed pond wells up with water from its cool depths,
and also receives rain from above
sent by the rain-god from time to time,
so that the rain from above and the spring water from below
mingle,
this pond will become washed through and radiant with fresh
water.
No part of it will be dark, stagnant, or blind.
In the same way,
a meditator practicing mindfulness of her body sensations
with equanimity
drenches her body with awareness,
so that no place remains unobserved,
and she moves her mind fluidly
from top to bottom and bottom to top
saturated with imperturbability.

All people feel fear.
Even the Buddha, before his enlightenment, had to struggle.
He said:
I used to live in the jungle, surrounded by feelings of anxiety.
Wild animals would approach, or the wind would shake the
trees.
Every time a branch fell I shuddered.
I thought to myself, why do I live constantly expecting
bad things to happen?
It was true, that while I walked in the jungle
worry and foreboding followed me;
when I stood still
worry and foreboding surrounded me like a cloud;
when I lay down
worry and foreboding covered me,
and when I sat down to meditate,
worry and foreboding hovered like mist.

We are told that due to his fear,
the Buddha became determined to arouse tireless energy
in unremitting effort
to gain insight into his suffering.
He concentrated his mind, he established mindfulness,
and slowly, and with great effort,
his mind became purified, bright,
under his control,
malleable, like properly heated gold,
wieldy, like the sword he used to carry,
steady and imperturbable like a Buddha.
The first true knowledge he attained
was the realization of equanimity.
It was his fear that goaded him towards liberation.

We should be modest, but not to a fault.
It is also healthy to acknowledge our own virtues.
Remind yourself of moments when you have helped
yourself and others.
Remember when you were openhanded, charitable,
giving and sharing your money
and your heart.
We know that you have welcomed
many meditating friends into your home.

We should try to avoid the habit
of passing judgment on other people.
Not all of another person's accomplishments or problems
are fully visible to us.
Someone may be gentle and pleasant,
but fearful.
Another person is equally pleasant,
free from fear, but lies.
These two people appear similar but have different depths,
like two ponds.

Similarly, two people may be equally quick
to anger, pride and greed,
but one of them also has some degree
of warmth and generosity.
If you are a hasty critic of people,
you will see these two as being alike.
Happily married people can become highly developed,
and so can single people,
because attainments and vulnerabilities are multiple.
No one trait or accomplishment defines a person.
Someone who is verbose, irritable, and vain
may also possess insight
that ensures progress in spite of shortcomings.

The greatest wisdom
is to perceive everyone around you
in their unique qualities, strengths and limitations.
Disarm your stereotypes and rapid judgments,
and recognize everyone in his or her fullness.
This practice of accurately noting everyone around you
will make you kinder, more realistic,
and will deepen your own grasp on human nature, including
your own.

The Dhamma is described as being plainly visible,
because if we are filled with hatred,
we know it;
and when hatred isn't present
that is also immediately experienced by us.
We can easily see some aspects of Dhamma in ourselves.
When fear lifts we feel it
in our mind and in our body.

But illusion can blind us.
The thought, "I know,"
is like opening the door to a haunted house.
We should always be asking ourselves whether
we really know what we think we do,
and upon what basis we claim our knowledge.
We should avoid becoming like the people
who follow in herds,
or like the people who are convinced of their own beliefs,
and who become blinded to discovery.

It is helpful if we think:
My goal is to become agreeable
to all of my companions in the life of meditation,
respected and esteemed by them.
My goal is to live according to precepts,
and to find security and insight
in my own mind
by conquering discontent, anger, and fear.
I hope that the people who have served me
by donating to centers where I have meditated
have gotten from my practice
the fruits that they deserve.

Our progress is gradual
and not always visible to us.
There is no abrupt way.
When we walk into the ocean we find
it inclines and slopes down,
gradually deepening.

When an outdoorsman uses an axe,
the handle begins to show the marks
of his finger, palm, and thumb,
and the hardwood erodes, without his being able to pinpoint
any single moment when these changes happened.
The meditative life leads to the wearing away of old patterns
even though we can't always assign a time or date
to our progress.

Our meditation is worthwhile even if it only leads to our
developing
the amount of Metta that lasts as long as it takes us to open
our eyes.
If we feel we can pervade the entire world around us
with Metta,
we have already achieved a divine stage.
It is said that the Buddha
once permeated the universe
with the feeling of loving kindness
for seven years.

When we feel kind thoughts we automatically feel well-being.

The experienced meditator
pervades all directions around her
with feelings of loving kindness,
everywhere,
to all beings including herself;
she pervades all the orbits of the galaxies
with loving kindness
that is abundant, exalted, and illimitable.
In her heart there are no barriers to her Metta.
She does this again with
compassion, joy, and equanimity.

Whatever we habitually think about
will form the tendencies and patterns of our mind.
When we incline our minds
towards the wellbeing of other people
then those tendencies
will arise more often,
putting us at ease.

When the crops are still growing in the fields,
the cowherd has to monitor his herd diligently,
to prevent them from consuming next year's food.
Similarly, our roaming minds require firm control.
But just as in the last months of summer,
when all the crops
have been harvested from the fields and stored in villages,
a cowherd can guard his cows merely by resting in the shade
of a tree
and keeping an eye on them,
in the same way,
when we have harvested kind thoughts,
we can observe our minds and bodies during meditation
in a relaxed manner.

When the Buddha referred to himself
he usually used the term, "Tathagata."
This ancient title refers
to his having emerged into the world
without craving,
and to his readiness to depart from the world
without clinging or regret.
He emerged and departed as all natural phenomena do,
an embodiment of nature.
He is present in the story,
talking face to face with living people,
making it clear how everything in the universe,
himself included,
arises and passes away.

The Tathagata is someone who understands
cause and effect.
He knows that our actions sculpt our future.
Actions are the birthplace of our character,
and are the seeds of the next moment.
We are the legatees of our own endeavors.

Because we may not live long enough
to know the full impact of everything we have done,
we can measure our choices best
by observing the effects they have
on our minds.
Do our actions make beneficent states grow?

Because we emerge from an endlessly ancient past,
and because we have so many thoughts in every moment,
we arise from and generate cascades of thought-actions.
The big events in our lives spring up from multiple actions
that have been added together,
subtracted from each other,
multiplied, compounded, or modified by each other.
Each moment has its cause but the cause is rarely singular.
Each one of us is a jungle of cause and effect,
from which we are hoping to grow
sturdy towering trees
of equanimity.

Four important steps that lead to
happiness and welfare for meditators are:
perfecting skillful and effective ways to earn your living;
protecting and guarding the wealth you have earned;
making friends on the Path who are established in
virtue, generosity, and resilient adaptation to life;
living with balance,
neither extravagantly nor overly cautiously.

There are four more things that guide meditators towards
happiness.
First, there is confidence that
the Buddha's Path leads towards wellbeing.
Second, is respecting all living beings,
and protecting the weak ones.
Third, is creating a home,
where there is delight in giving and sharing.
Remember that your own economic competence is essential
for your householder's journey.
Finally, there is the wisdom of understanding impermanence.

In the same way that all the rivers of the world flow down to
the sea,
wind down to the sea, and give their water up to it,
so too the Buddha's teachings all flow down towards
and become one with Nibbana.
Both people who are single, and people who enjoy
the married life of sensual pleasures,
are capable of flowing towards Nibbana,
because the current of Dhamma floats everyone
who is in it
to the same shoreless ocean.

It was recorded that in the ancient days,
meditators living in hermitages
had to carry their water uphill from the river
in heavy pots.
Whenever anyone noticed that the pots of water had become
low,
it was his job to replenish them.
But if the pots were too heavy for him,
he would silently gesture with a signal of the hand
to someone else,
and then the two men would haul the pot
by lifting it,
all four hands together
in silence.

How do we know when we are meditating properly?
When we are living in concord, with mutual appreciation,
without disputing,
blending like ocean, shore, and sand,
viewing each other with acceptance and generosity.
Is your meditation pulsing friendship
like waves?

Find noble friends, companions, and associates,
with whom you can share conversation about meditation
in natural, unspoiled and peaceful environments.
Frequenting assemblies where Dhamma is discussed
on land that is dedicated
to walking the Path
is a way to both be inspired, and to inspire others.
We have friends among people, and we have friends among
birds, trees, and streams.

The Tathagata was not worried whether he was liberating
the whole world.
He focused on teaching freedom from ignorance,
and purification of the mind through meditation.
The word, Dhamma, and the word, purification,
refer to those practices that lead beyond sorrow,
because they restore the clear and unbiased mind.

The Tathagata explained what he knew
regardless of the size of his audience.
He did not worry whether he was acceptable
or popular.

Just as a ripening thunderhead ascends
high into the atmosphere
at the end of a drought,
and pours life back into the shriveled crops,
in the same way there are people who arise
in this world
who shower goodness, and happiness
on many people.

Consider a man or a woman
lost on a lonely mountain range,
who stumbled upon an ancient path,
an ancient trail,
trod by the feet of travelers long ago,
and he or she turned onto it,
and followed this footpath through the wilderness,
until he or she found an ancient city,
a sacred wheel-shaped ground,
where wise rulers once held court,
with palaces, observatories,
meadows and flowering groves,
surrounded by stone walls
placed by generations of loving hands;
in the same way the Tathagata, too,
found the original path for crossing the mountain ranges,
traversing the dark forest,
the one and only way
worn by the feet
of the fully enlightened ones of old.

One evening when the Buddha was growing old,
he sat with his back warming in the rays of the setting sun.
Ananda massaged his limbs
and noticed that his skin was no longer clear and bright;
his arms and legs were weak and blotched;
and his spine was bowed over like a tired old man.

He changed his position to rest his back against a pillar,
and he told Ananda,
"My back is uncomfortable, I need to rest it."
Then he folded his worn robes and lay down
on his right side
like a lion,
alert and fully aware.

The Buddha has said:
I have taught the Dhamma, keeping nothing secret,
and saying nothing esoteric.
The Tathagata teaches with an open hand,
holding nothing back, revealing everything,
grasping nothing in a fist.
If there is anyone who thinks,
"All meditators from now on should refer to me as their
teacher,"
let him say so.
But a Tathagata does not think like that.

The Tathagata did not know
or claim to foresee
the future of his dispensation.
Like the rain cloud,
he scattered his teaching everywhere around him.
The grass will grow differently
in each of the next generations.

Constantly referring to a teacher,
or flattering his name
is not a way to pay him your respects.
A meditator pays homage to the Buddha,
by meditating, living the virtuous life,
and building a community of like-minded friends.
To pay homage to the Buddha,
be equanimous, free from turmoil, contented,
a vessel of gladness.

In the end, the Buddha said:

I am now old and worn out, someone who has walked the long

trail to its end;

I have made it to my honored eightieth year.

Just as an old horse is helped to hobble forward by having

knee braces and ankle braces wrapped around his weakened

joints,

in the same way the Tathagata's body is kept going by

bandages and straps.

Therefore live as islands on your own.

Live as lights of your own wisdom.

Be your own refuge,

with Dhamma as your island and your light.

Wander the world for the benefit of all, for the happiness of
all,
out of compassion for the lonely
and the lost,
for the wellbeing and happiness
of gods and people.
Dare to walk alone, unaccompanied,
teaching that which is true
at its beginning, middle, and end,
the same in letter and spirit,
the same in words and actions.

Teach the holy life by living it.

Notes

In the process of compiling *In the Spirit of the Buddha* we have consulted the following texts:

The Middle Length Discourses of the Buddha: A Translation of the Majjhima Nikāya; trans. Bhikkhu Ñāṇamoli and Bhikkhu Bodhi; Wisdom, Boston 1995.

The Long Discourses of the Buddha: A Translation of the Digha Nikāya; trans. Maurice Walshe; Wisdom, Boston 1987.

The Numerical Discourses of the Buddha: An Anthology of Suttas from the Aṅguttara Nikāya; trans. Bhikkhu Bodhi; Buddhist Pub. Soc., Kandy, Sri Lanka 1999.

Udāna and Itivuttaka: Two Classics from the Pali Canon; trans. John D. Ireland; Buddhist Pub. Soc., Kandy, Sri Lanka 1997.

The Life of the Buddha; Bhikkhu Ñāṇamoli, Buddhist Pub. Soc., Kandy, Sri Lanka 1972.

ABOUT PARIYATTI

Pariyatti is dedicated to providing affordable access to authentic teachings of the Buddha about the Dhamma theory (*pariyatti*) and practice (*paṭipatti*) of Vipassana meditation. A 501(c)(3) nonprofit charitable organization since 2002, Pariyatti is sustained by contributions from individuals who appreciate and want to share the incalculable value of the Dhamma teachings. We invite you to visit www.pariyatti.org to learn about our programs, services, and ways to support publishing and other undertakings.

Pariyatti Publishing Imprints

Vipassana Research Publications (focus on Vipassana as taught by S.N. Goenka in the tradition of Sayagyi U Ba Khin)

BPS Pariyatti Editions (selected titles from the Buddhist Publication Society, copublished by Pariyatti in the Americas)

Pariyatti Digital Editions (audio and video titles, including discourses)

Pariyatti Press (classic titles returned to print and inspirational writing by contemporary authors)

Pariyatti enriches the world by

- disseminating the words of the Buddha,
- providing sustenance for the seeker's journey,
- illuminating the meditator's path.

www.ingramcontent.com/pod-product-compliance
Lightning Source LLC
Chambersburg PA
CBHW041427090426
42741CB00002B/59